DATE DUE

DIVING AND SNORKELING GUIDE TO

Australia

Coral Sea and Great Barrier Reef

Carl Roessler

51195

9 781559 920445

Pisces Books
A Division of Gulf Publishing Company
Houston, Texas

Dedication

To Jessica,
Who makes all things possible.

Library of Congress Cataloging-in-Publication Data

Roessler, Carl, 1933-
  Diving and snorkeling guide to Australia, Coral Sea and Great
Barrier Reef / Carl Roessler.
      p.   cm.
  ISBN 1-55992-044-0
  1. Skin diving—Australia—Guide-books. 2. Skin diving—
Coral Sea—Guide-books. 3. Skin diving—Australia—Great
Barrier Reef (Qld.)—Guide-books. 4. Scuba diving—Australia
—Guide-books. 5. Scuba diving—Coral Sea—Guide-books.
6. Scuba diving—Australia—Great Barrier Reef (Qld.)—
Guidebooks. 7. Australia—Description and travel—1981—
Guide-books. 8. Coral Sea Region—Description and travel—
Guide-books. 9. Great Barrier Reef Region (Qld.)—Description
and travel—Guide-books. I. Title.
GV840.S78R58   1991
797.2'3—dc20   90-20576
                                                        CIP

Printed in Hong Kong

10 9 8 7 6 5 4 3 2 1

Table of Contents

Preface

This book is a labor of love for me. Since 1972, I have made twenty-eight cruises to Australia's Coral Sea. Profound adventures and magnificent marine life are waiting for those willing to cruise hundreds of miles to reach these remote reefs.

For all those years, the Coral Sea has been one of the two or three best diving adventures in the world.

It is a pleasure for me to share these exotic reefs with you, in hopes that you too may experience their wonders.

Carl Roessler

A diver encounters a school of jacks in the shallow water above this Coral Sea pinnacle.

Blue-head wrasse and soft coral are some of the exotically colored and beautiful Coral Sea dwellers.

◄

Large gorgonian fans are characteristic of the valleys between pinnacles at Marion, Flinders, and Lihou Reefs. Currents are funneled through the valleys to create perfect feeding grounds for these stately coral colonies.

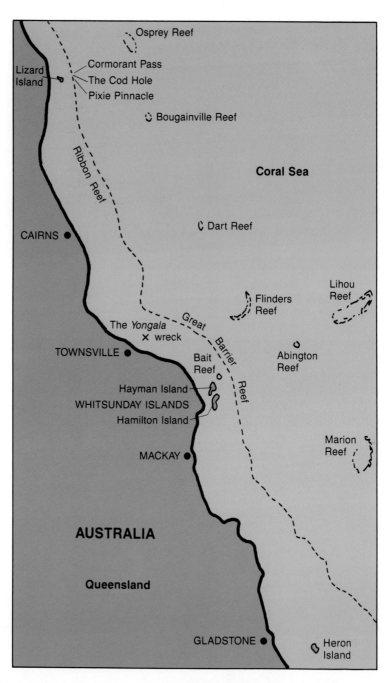

Australia's northeastern coast: the Great Barrier Reef and the Coral Sea.

How to Use This Guide

This guide was developed to familiarize you with the location and terrain of the principal dive sites of Australia's Queensland Coast and Coral Sea. Australia's tropical dive region is so vast that you will find this guide far less precise than a guide to, say, the Cayman Islands; one good reason is that there is no one who has dived all of the thousands of available sites in some 360,000 square miles of this region. Another reason is that many of the precise locations are known only to individual boat captains who jealously guard their proprietary knowledge. This is particularly true at the Coral Sea atolls such as Marion, Lihou, and Moore reefs.

You should be aware that some magazine writers and boat captains will go out and arbitrarily assign names to sites for their own convenience, for example, in writing an article. When you arrive and use those names, the boat captain you are with may be mystified because he was not with that writer. Rather than use that dubious technique, I prefer to describe

Divers enter the water off Diamond Island.

an area so any captain might recognize the place you are seeking. Parenthetically, it is also true that when every anchorage has a cute name assigned that everyone knows, the diving will have significantly declined in quality.

Another consideration on these massive reefs is that no two captains will drop their anchors on precisely the same spot; thus the underwater features you see can be different even at a named site. For example, out at Marion reef there are clusters of several enormous pinnacles; whether you anchor at the northern or southern end would completely change your perception of that site. If you and another diver from a different cruise talked, each of you might not recognize that same cluster from the other's description.

Whenever you are diving these sites you will be diving with a dive service and will not be required to find the site yourself; your guide or captain will give you a good idea as to depth, currents, topography, and photo subjects.

The Rating System for Divers and Dives

Our suggestions of the minimum level of expertise required for any given dive should be taken conservatively, keeping in mind the old adage about there being old divers and bold divers, but few old, bold divers. We consider a novice to be someone in decent physical condition who has recently completed a basic certification diving course, or a certified diver who has not been diving recently or who has no experience in similar waters. An intermediate diver, in this system, would be someone with between 50 and 150 dives; valuable experience, but perhaps not enough to cope with unexpected difficulties. We consider an advanced diver to be someone who has completed an advanced certification diving course, has been diving recently in similar water, and is in excellent physical condition. You will have to decide if you are capable of making any particular dive, depending on your level of training, recentness of experience, and physical condition, as well as water conditions at the site. Remember that water conditions can change at any time. It is important not to overrate your skills when diving at major sites in Australia. Some sites on the Great Barrier Reef are known for the currents that can be running, while some Coral Sea reefs offer sheer, deep walls. One positive factor is that most reef sites offered to visiting divers have shallow tops (i.e., these mature reefs reach to within ten feet or less of the surface).

In the Coral Sea, crinoids provide occasional bursts of brilliant color near the shallow tops of coral pinnacles. ▶

These large gorgonian fans are characteristic of the valleys between pinnacles at Marion, Flinders, and Lihou. These valleys apparently funnel the currents to create perfect feeding for these stately colonies of coral.

Even experienced divers are careful to monitor depth time, air supply, and decompression requirements throughout each excursion.

I have organized the guide by area as follows:

1. The Great Barrier Reef: locations out of Cairns, Cooktown, or Port Douglas in the north.
2. The Great Barrier Reef: locations out of Townsville in the south.
3. The northern Coral Sea reefs: Bougainville and Osprey reefs.
4. The central Coral Sea: Dart, Flinders, Abington, Diamond, Holmes, Moore, and Lihou reefs.
5. The southern Coral Sea: Marion Reef.

Each of these regions, indeed each of these reefs, is larger than most Caribbean islands. Divers whose prior experience has been limited to the Caribbean will find that distances in the Pacific dwarf those of the Caribbean. This confers obvious benefits such as greater variety of dive sites and less pressure on the more distant ones; on the other hand, these are distinct disadvantages for those who are limited in time, or who have difficulty with long boat rides.

Since diving services in Australia are evolving rapidly, I have tried not to make the text dependent upon them. The most important contributions I can make are to give you insights into what makes Australia's diving unique, and where its most important reefs are located. It is my hope that you will then have the pleasure of "pioneering" Australia's great reefs for yourself.

Wherever currents flow, as here in the gutters of Osprey Reef, the walls bloom with colorful corals.

1

Overview of Australia

Until less than 400 years ago, Australia was unknown to the rest of the world. Its vast empty expanses had been populated for 40,000 years by bands of aboriginals who had come from Asia by sea. Some traders may have travelled from Indonesia, but Australia's physical and political isolation were complete. A map produced by the astronomer/scholar Ptolemy dating from the second century A.D. shows an immense southern landmass known as Terra Incognita, the unknown land. In the early

Island and Bay at Lizard Island, northward from Cairns.

This moray eel is being attended by a cleaner wrasse.

seventeenth century, the explorations of Dutch and Portuguese navigators began to define the actual shape and extent of Australia, and the name on the landmass became Terra Australis. In 1606, Luis Vaez de Torres sailed through the strait between Australia and Papua New Guinea that now bears his name. The Dutch captains Janszoon and Carstensz explored long expanses of the northern and western coasts. The first Englishman to reach the continent was a buccaneer, William Dampier, in 1688. By this time Terra Australis had become New Holland.

European civilization was moving in on Australia and a great tragedy was to be enacted. All across the Pacific and the Far East, the arrival of Europeans bearing unfamiliar diseases wiped out millions of native inhabitants. Moreover, the culture of conquest which pushed back frontiers claimed many who were in the way. The aboriginals, it would turn out, got in the way.

The aboriginal inhabitants of this new continent lived lives of physical privation and hardship, yet shared an astonishingly rich body of culture and myth. They had an elaborate relationship with their ancestors ("the

Here and there on a healthy reef, one will find massive crown-of-thorns starfish (Acanthaster planci).

Creators"); every physical feature of the landscape around them could be linked back to the creators through stories and rituals handed down over countless generations. Collectively, the myths and legend are known as the Dreamtime lore. Travelers to Australia may find books on this remarkable heritage a source of awe and wonder.

The tragedy of the aboriginals was that their culture depended upon an unchanging environment, and European conquest has always meant overwhelming change.

Today, the problems of the aboriginals are depressingly similar to those of the American Indians, lost and purposeless on the continent they once owned. Despite the type of welfare programs modern governments seem to proliferate, alcohol and other scourges plague the aboriginals.

The first European settlement in Australia occurred in 1788, when British captain Arthur Philip established a colony near Sydney. As late as 200 years ago there were a mere thousand Europeans and some 300,000 aboriginals sharing a continent similar in landmass to the United States. The European population grew steadily, from 2.25 million in 1881 to 7.4 million in 1945. In the period following World War II, a major immigration program doubled the population by 1984. In one of the greatest immigration movements in history, 4.2 million settlers from 120 countries flooded into Australia. While Britain and Ireland provided the vast majority, significant populations from Italy, Greece, the Netherlands, Germany, New Zealand, Poland, the U.S., Vietnam, and Lebanon swelled the throng.

Because Australia is the world's driest continent, vast areas of semidesert inhibit settlement. As a result, Australia's relatively small population of fifteen million crowds into eight state and territory capitals, and less than 15% of the people live in rural areas.

Australia is a young country. One need only review the original settlement dates of capital cities of the various states to illustrate this: Hobart, Tasmania–1803; Brisbane, Queensland–1824; Perth, Western Australia–1829; Melbourne, Victoria–1835; and Adelaide, South Australia–1836. These early settlements were the starting points for further exploration and settlement.

One key problem in early Australia was to find a base for an economy. Australia's first purpose had been as a penal colony; by 1840 Britain had sent 100,000 convicts to this far-off island continent. Early governors

Even rainbow runners, a normally shy fish, mill about human intruders without fear.

were empowered to grant land free to anyone willing to take over the tasks of employing and feeding the convicts. Early efforts involved whaling and sealing, harvesting the natural wealth of the seas around Australia's immense coastline. Large-scale agriculture was not successful because of the aridity of much of the country. We can only speculate today how Australia might have been had it been blessed with a temperate climate and rich soil.

History actually turned on experiments conducted on breeding Merino sheep known for their fine wool. Merinos were imported from the hot, dry plains of Spain. From their original importation in 1796, the sheep, and the wool industry they supported, became the base of Australia's economy.

As more free settlers came to Australia, they raised fierce objections to the continuing transport of convicts to their new land. By 1853 only western Australia accepted new prisoners, and by 1868 the use of Australia as a penal colony had ended.

In 1851 the discovery of gold in New South Wales and Victoria drew an immense influx of new settlers. The process of transforming Australia to a governed nation began. Between 1850 and 1891 the six Australian colonies were empowered to form legislatures and frame constitutions. Between 1891 and 1901 a series of conferences fashioned the former colonies into states under a federal constitution. The first parliament of the new nation convened on April 29, 1901.

On the coral reefs one may get close to strikingly decorated fish such as the right-angle butterflyfish (Chaetodon auriga).

Australia Today

Modern Australia is a sometimes confusing mixture of old and new. In her steel-and-glass-towered cities the entire world is a computer keystroke away. Yet her small towns and vast outback have changed very little. One need only fly across the vast, dry central plains to Ayers Rock to realize how little of Australia's immense space is populated. Like the United States, Australia has astonishing physical contrasts: the tropical beaches and islands of Queensland's Great Barrier Reef and the towering cliffs and cold waters of South Australia are as distinctly opposite as the beaches of Florida and the granite coast of Maine.

Australia's enormous mineral resources, from gold to uranium, have provided wealth beyond measure. Her newest industry, tourism, has enjoyed periods of boom and recesssion as various internal and external factors exerted influence. For example, a period of falling airfares following airline deregulation began a travel boom. Frantic development began in Queensland, severely testing the country's ability to develop a tourist infrastructure. A tradition of strong socialistic unions have constantly hobbled these efforts. Over the past two decades every trip I have enjoyed to Australia was shadowed by another public-sector union on strike. While these strikes are an inconvenience to travelers, their extent and recurrence have been a substantial factor in Australia's not reaching her potential in tourism, and perhaps as a nation.

Weather

Cyclone season lasts from January through March and is very reminiscent of the hurricane season in the Caribbean. Because of the great size of the Queensland coast/Great Barrier Reef, cyclones may not intersect your path during a vacation; still, their possible occurrence, coupled with the fact that there are few islands in the good dive areas, inhibits boat traffic to the distant Coral Sea reefs. A dive boat caught out in the Coral Sea may have a two-day run to reach the coast. Discretion being by far the better part of valor, smart captains work within the Great Barrier Reef during these months. Between cyclones the weather will be calm and fine, just as in the Caribbean between hurricanes. When you have spent months planning and anticipating your trip, however, the unpredictability of the cyclones might influence you to choose another time of year.

April, May, and June are generally the time of the trade winds, brisk sea breezes which can cause dive boats a rather rocky ride. Sites such as that of the *Yongala* wreck south of Townsville can be impossible during

Like a huge butterfly, a stingray soars in the shadow of the Yongala.

this time. Similarly, while some boats do go out into the Coral Sea, these can be memorable rides. Once you have reached the lee side of a reef the diving can be fine, however; so trips taken during these months can be reasonably successful, if physical.

July, August, and September begin the prime weather season. There can be periods of excellent weather in July and August when a boat cruise is as smooth as that of an airliner. This is also an excellent period for sightings of some of the larger animals.

Over the years, October and November have been excellent, at least in terms of percentages. There are no guarantees about Australian weather. There is a big ocean out there, and it can blow up at any time. Still, on average these are excellent months.

There appears to have been a climatic shift over the past two decades, wherein the best weather has tended to occur earlier. In the early 1970s, October through December was prime time; now professionals recommend July to November as the best percentage time for a cruise. While all this may seem unnecessarily complicated, limited shelter makes the Coral Sea a place where weather can have a profound impact on your dive vacation. I have personally made twenty-six cruises out into the Coral Sea as of this writing. I still can't be sure that a See & Sea cruise that I escort will not run into wind and bumpy seas . . .

Hotels

Hotel facilities for divers are an interesting subject in Australia. First, it must be said that there are hundreds of hotels along the Queensland coast, and even several out among the islands of the Great Barrier Reef. With few exceptions, however, it must also be said that the diving within reach of most shore facilities is not the diving that made Australia famous.

For the most part, the great dive sites occur in distant places where there are no hotels. More than any other place in the world, this is live-aboard country. However, hotels for extra days before or after a cruise can be wonderful. In addition, those who do not have the time or money during their visit to see the distant reefs may be perfectly happy with the diving experiences closer to the mainland.

The major hotels advertising to attract divers boil down to four: Heron, Lizard, Hayman, and Hamilton Islands. These four facilities are about as different as they can be.

A flowery cod (Epinephelus fuscoguttatus) *is so curious and unafraid that it peers intensely at the camera from point-blank range as the picture is taken.*

Heron Island is an active resort built on a bird sanctuary; it was the first island to advertise for divers, and the first to develop hand-fed fish on the nearby coral heads as an entertainment. Heron is in the southern Great Barrier Reef, off the city of Gladstone.

Lizard Island is an overnight cruise or one-hour flight north of Cairns, and began life as a fishing camp for the "old boy network" of Australia. On my first visit to Lizard Island Resort I recommended that air-conditioning be installed. The look I received in return cast me (and by implication, Americans in general) firmly into the wimp category. Big game fishermen have long dominated Lizard, leaving a secondary role for divers. Still, Lizard is the only island of the four to be within reach of a world-class dive, the Cod Hole.

Hayman Island is a posh watering hole for the international jet set, isolated on its own island. An hour away, by fast boat, are modest reefs, but Hayman is best enjoyed as a sybaritic refuge after a dive cruise.

Hamilton was designed as a complete community: high-rise hotels, fishing village, sprawling condos. Its activities range from tennis and golf to helicopter diving at reefs such as Bait Reef, which is also used by Hayman Island.

All of these hotels are interesting, but all are far from Australia's best dive sites.

Transportation

Taxicabs and rental cars are well established in Queensland; at airports in Cairns and Townsville both are available upon arrival. One caution would be this: Australia is heavily unionized with a strong socialistic tradition. You may sometimes encounter workers such as taxi drivers in service industries whose idea of service is not at all what a visitor might hope. Some Americans are shocked by this, as we expect everyone to be cheerful and helpful. Don't be surprised, and your vacation won't be dampened by occasional "wankers" (a pejorative local term for jerks).

Foreign Exchange, Dining, and Shopping

Currency: The Australian dollar has had a wide range of values against the U.S. dollar over the years. At the time of this writing it hovers in the .74-.80 range. U.S. dollars thus seem strong when you convert them to Australian currency. In most cities of any size credit cards are widely accepted; for most dive cruises you will have paid in advance, so your Australian money transactions are usually limited to shopping or dining.

A barramundi cod (Cromilepsis altivelus) *peers from a break in the hull of the* Yongala.

One caveat: You will receive the official exchange rate if you convert your dollars at a bank, but hotels and restaurants charge a hefty fee.

Dining: Sydney is like San Francisco in being a mecca for gourmands. From oysters to John Dory, from Barramundi to meat pies, the fare is varied and delicious. Other cities such as Brisbane, Cairns, and Townsville also boast fine restaurants. The island continent has a strong fare of seafood to please the most demanding palate; add the international cuisine offered by generations of immigrants and traveling divers can enjoy Indonesian, Thai, Italian, French, German, and a variety of other dishes.

Shopping: Australia's shopping is a cornucopia of Aussie treasures — Kangaroo skin alone is found in a stunning variety of souvenirs. Meanwhile sheepskin and sheepskin products are fine values, as well as bringing

back fond memories. Opals offer opportunities for appreciation while you enjoy their exotic, unique beauty. A black opal from the Lightning Ridge mines is a rare and wondrous treasure.

Besides Diving

Australia is a treasure-house of images for the traveler; gleaming cities, astonishing seacoasts, the Blue Mountains, an arid scrubland interior desert, geologic wonders such as Ayers Rock and the Olgas. The only pity is that with our passion for diving we never have the time or money to really see Australia. Be assured that whatever extra time you can spend in this fantastic country will reward you for a lifetime.

Customs and Immigration

Like most modern nations, Australia is simplifying immigration requirements. Present or send your U.S. passport to an Australian consulate; they will (as of this writing) stamp it with a visa good for multiple entries over a period of 5 years.

On the plane approaching Australia you will receive two forms. One is for customs, and will outline stringent rules against bringing any foodstuffs into Australia that could carry agricultural pests or viruses. The penalties are quite severe for violating these rules. The second form records your name, passport numbers, when and where your visa was issued, and asks a few questions on matters such as how much currency you are carrying. Upon arrival at the first Australian airport, your documents will be checked and stamped.

◄ *The elegant Moorish idol* (Zanclus cornutus) *often occurs in social groups on the pinnacles.*

2

Diving in Australia

The first important thing to understand is that Australia is a massive continent, and that its diving ranges from warm to cold, near to far, magnificent to poor. American divers can easily understand that on an island continent the size of the United States, Australia will have diving contrasts between its regions just as Florida, New England, and California have contrasts.

For purposes of this guide we are considering the Queensland (i.e., the northeastern, tropical) coast. This coast is guarded by the 1,200-mile

An outburst of red gorgonians in a coral canyon.

Some fans have small polyps; others have polyps with longer tentacles which produce a "soft" or fuzzy visual effect.

Great Barrier Reef. This colossal coral structure can be visualized as a broad, shallow plateau with scattered hieroglyphics of reef. In many areas these reefs are so complex they have not even been charted, and even the Australian Navy avoids them. In the passages between these twisted reefs I have seen 8-knot currents which can be very interesting if you are on a dive cruiser that does 8 knots . . .

The outer edges of the plateau are lined with reefs that border on the open Coral Sea. In the area north of Cairns, and off Port Douglas and Cooktown, these are known as the "Ribbon Reefs." Indeed, on nautical charts you will see them referred to as "Ribbon Reef #1," "Ribbon Reef #2," etc. There is a broad shipping channel within the reef for ships moving up and down the coast. Visiting divers must factor travel time to sites on the Great Barrier Reef and Coral Sea into vacation plans. In my professional career I own the world's largest travel agency exclusively devoted to divers, See & Sea Travel, of San Francisco. Since 1972 my company has arranged dive vacations for many thousands of Australia-bound divers. I can tell you from long personal experience that Australia stands apart from all of the other world-class destinations in being misunderstood. The problem is straightforward: Australia's diving is so scattered that a diver should make a commitment of a week or more to see even a sampling of the great sites. I get many calls from people who have scheduled two or three free days to sample Australia's great diving. Getting them to understand that there will be 12 hours by boat to reach the first reef often shocks them, but that is part of diving Australia's Queensland coast.

Australia has disappointed many divers who did not fully comprehend how remote the great diving is, or how weak the convenient diving is. As a general rule, the diving that made Australia famous, and where the crystal clear pictures were taken for magazines, are not on the Great Barrier Reef at all; they lie 150-320 miles out to sea on the great oceanic reefs.

While the Great Barrier Reef has all of the species of marine life, and certain spectacular sites such as the Cod Hole and *Yongala* wreck, it is plagued with strong currents, turbid water, dead coral, and seasonally windy weather.

More than any other dive destination in the world, Australia penalizes the naive and the uninformed. Divers have arrived in Cairns or Townsville and expected the great diving to be as convenient as at some Caribbean island. Woe betide those who do not learn the unavoidable choices with which Australia challenges the unwary. Many in Australia have taken

The clown triggerfish (Balistoides conspicillum) *is one of the most intelligent and aggressive fish on any reef.*

The crinoid (Comanthina) *folds its feeding arms when the current stops.*

my comments as critical or even negative. The truth is that informed divers who spend the needed time and money to see Australia's greatest reefs will consider them (as I do) some of the world's best. On the other hand, those who simply believe all of the ubiquitous advertising for the Great Barrier Reef could be disappointed with 30-50 ft visibility, strong currents, and ugly underwater scenery. My fear, and certainly my experience to date, is that those uninformed divers will return home and bitterly denounce Australia as a whole.

You may feel I am overly stressing this point, but consider this truth: Australia has victimized more divers than any other destination in the world, and has very mixed reviews among visiting divers. This has been a great loss for Australia and for traveling divers.

The oceanic reefs of the northern Coral Sea lie north and eastward from Lizard Island, which is itself north of Cairns. A live-aboard cruise to the two major reefs of the northern Coral Sea, Osprey and Bougainville Reefs, begins with an overnight cruise to the reefs east of Lizard Island. These are the northern Ribbon Reefs, and the site of two rich spots known as the Cod Hole and Pixie Pinnacle. While I have made clear my general impression of Great Barrier Reef diving, these two sites are sufficiently unusual to demand inclusion.

3

The Northern Great Barrier Reef

The Cod Hole

Typical depth range	:	30-80 feet (10-27 meters)
Typical current conditions	:	None to strong
Expertise required	:	Novice or better
Access	:	Boat

This dive site is one of those rare wonders of diving's great past which is now, alas, being visited by hordes of divers. The Cod Hole lies just

At the Cod Hole, constant feeding of fish has made them fearless. Here a large moray eel swims freely about looking for food.

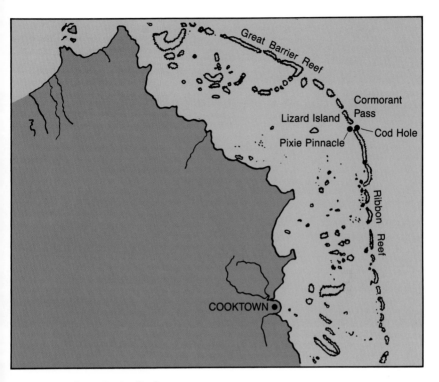

The northern Great Barrier Reef.

inside the mouth of Cormorant Pass, on the south side of the pass. Here it is protected behind the northern end of Ribbon Reef no. 10.

The Cod Hole an enchanted place whose origins are quite humble. Fishermen came here for years because it offered protection from wind and wave. As they cleaned their catches, these fishermen would throw scraps and innards overboard, while below, the large groupers which fed in the pass ate the scraps and grew fat. The groupers became conditioned to eating food whose source was man; it was a modest transition to divers hand-feeding them. For a wonderful few years the Cod Hole was an almost private preserve. Few boats went there and the divers who got in the water with the big fish the Australians call potato cod were uniquely blessed. The Cod Hole is a reef area perhaps 150 yards in length. The coral is not very impressive: some ledges and patch reefs ranging from 30-80 feet in depth. When you are in the water at the Cod Hole you will recognize the shape of the pass, or channel, between reefs. Your dive boat's mooring will be in shallow water on the northern edge of the reef. The coral terrain then slopes down in several shelves along the southern side of the pass. Most of the diving is done in 30-60 feet of water among irregular rocky patches.

A small group of butterfly fish pass unconcernedly as Jessica Roessler, the author's wife, visits with a moray eel.

A pair of moray eels (Gymnothorax) watch the passing scene with every expectation of being fed.

A diver swims next to a large potato cod (Epinephelus Tukula) *at the Cod Hole.*

This would not be a particularly attractive dive site were it not for the tame animals. Now, there are divers who feel that feeding animals to tame them is a terrible practice, unnatural and even dangerous to marine life. In general I agree, and seldom feed fish. At the Cod Hole, what has been created is a marine zoo, which now has the full protection of National Park status. Some places in the world that act as zoos may offend purists, but are valuable to the public at large. Years of feeding have caused perhaps twenty potato cod, a few napoleon wrasse, three large green moray eels, and a number of other species such as flowery cod and greasy cod to simply gather around for a handout. In the old days when a single boat would put perhaps ten divers in the water it was pure enchantment. The animals would swarm over us offering photo opportunities beyond compare. This was a dive that had all the zest of a wild place, the action of a circus, and the personal interaction of a zoo, rolled into one. The world cannot leave such places alone, and before long the reputation of the Cod Hole spread.

At the same time, civilization was spreading northward from Cairns; now a parade of boats from Cairns, Port Douglas, and Cooktown converge upon the Cod Hole. With several groups of divers in the water the fish have a way of charging from one group to another. One moment you are surrounded by massive spectaculars; the next moment the fickle creatures have raced off to see if someone else is offering juicier handouts.

The Cod Hole is definitely one of those places you should experience. If you are fortunate you'll arrive on the first boat of the day, and enjoy the sublime pleasure of these magnificent creatures practically alone.

Since the Cod Hole is, as described earlier, in one of the passes through which tidal water flows in and out of the Great Barrier Reef, you may at times experience strong currents here. Be sure to consult the boat captain or dive guide before entering the water.

Pixie Pinnacle

Typical depth range	:	3-90 feet (1-30 meters)
Typical current conditions	:	None to strong
Expertise required	:	Novice or better
Access	:	Boat

South of the Cod Hole lies another unusual dive site known as "Pixie Pinnacle" or "Pixie Bommie." Bommie is an Australian slang term derived from the aboriginal word *Bombora,* denoting a coral structure that rises to, but does not pierce, the surface. Pixie is a splendid example of the formation; we also see many in the atoll lagoons of the Coral Sea.

This particular pinnacle rises vertically from a depth of at least 150 feet, the shallowest 60-70 feet of the structure has sides that are quite sheer. Further down, it slopes outward like the base of a mountain.

Pixie is located just inside a rather complicated pass through the outer reef. As we cruise up to Pixie we see a winding pass shaped almost like a river delta, doubtless shaped by similar hydrodynamic forces. Then, perhaps 100 yards from the inner edge of the reef is a tiny spot of yellow-green in the blue water: Welcome to Pixie. While the shape of

A nudibranch glides across the reef, flaring its wide skirt nearly every second.

A pair of clownfish (Premnas biaculeatus) *dance above the poisonous tentacles of their host anemone.*

the pass directs the strongest currents past this structure, the currents a diver feels can still be impressive. Oceanic currents deposit a myriad of living creatures around many structures (even wrecks) lying in their paths. At the bottom of the food chain are the free-drifting plankton and larval corals. The plankton provide a constant food stream, so that when the larval corals drop out of their pelagic state and take up residence on any pinnacle, they grow like weeds.

A diver can circle the entire pinnacle in a few minutes. The northern and western faces have galleries or ledges cut into the side of the cylinder where a collection of lionfish, groupers, corals, crinoids, fans, nudibranchs, and anemone/clownfish pairs are found. The eastern and southern faces are steep and sheer, and photographers proceed hand over hand like mountaineers, peering closely at each square foot of coral, looking for small treasures. Pixie is one of those wonder-filled places where the closer you look, the more there is to find.

In general, expect to shoot close-up photos, because visibility is often limited to 50-70 feet. If you are excited by nudibranchs, sailfin leaf fish, and other unusual species, prowling the surface of this pinnacle will

Clouds of fairy basslets (Anthias) *swarm in the open water a few feet from the protection of Pixie Pinnacle.*

reward your search with excellent photographic subjects. The rest is up to you . . .

Swarming in the open water about the pinnacle are countless thousands of fairy basslets *(Anthias)* and fusiliers *(Caesio)*. The visual effect of these immense numbers of small fish is overwhelming — sometimes they practically block one's view.

As in much of the interior of the Great Barrier Reef, turbid masses of tidal water churn past in two daily cycles. The bad news is poor visibility; the good news is that the ceaseless currents bring a constant stream of food to the pinnacle.

Like the Cod Hole, Pixie is visited far more often than such a small place can withstand. Slowly, the impact of divers is showing. Still, the miracle that nature creates when a combination of currents deposits vast quantities of life in one place endures here. For such a small structure, Pixie has a biomass that defies expectations. I have only seen one or two places in the world with anything like the profusion of marine creatures found here. Nudibranchs, rabbitfish, brilliant red clownfish — the unusual and exotic are here to be found.

A rabbitfish is among many species which throng about the pillar known as Pixie Pinnacle.

4

The Southern Great Barrier Reef

The Yongala Wreck

Typical depth range	:	45-90 feet (15-30 meters)
Typical current conditions	:	None to strong
Expertise required	:	Intermediate or better
Access	:	Boat

Located a few hours' steaming south of Townsville, the *Yongala* is one of three world-class dive sites on the Great Barrier Reef, the other

Jacks and batfish swirl around a diver on the Yongala's massive bulk.

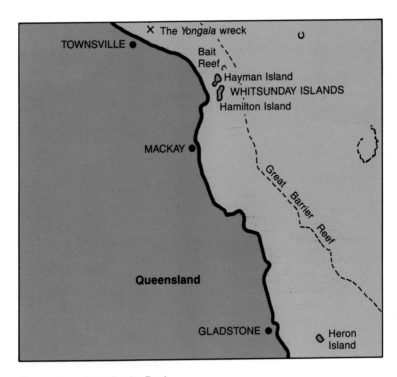

The southern Great Barrier Reef.

two, of course, being the Cod Hole and Pixie Pinnacle, 200 miles further north.

The *Yongala* was lost in a typhoon in 1911, and her whereabouts were unknown for many years. She lies on a broad, flat plain of sand that stretches unbroken for ten miles in every direction, right in the middle of the main north-south shipping channel. There are no convenient radar markers, so captains must sometimes search for hours to find her. At certain times of year there can be eight-foot seas above the *Yongala,* making diving impossible; this occurs mainly between February and June, but can happen any time.

It is also important to point out that occasionally powerful currents sweep across this wreck with such force that unwary divers could have their masks torn off.

I mention these conditions so no one will think that the *Yongala* is an easy dive. Yes, I have made these dives in perfect conditions — visibility of more than 50 feet (we could snorkel on the surface and see the hull 45 feet below us) and no current. Two hours later, a raging current set in . . .

Rays are frequently seen around the Yongala.

Because the *Yongala* is the only large structure on the bottom, all manner of creatures have flocked to it. The wreck lies on its starboard side, pointing north. The sandy bottom is at 90 feet, and the shallowest portion of the wreck is 45 feet beneath the surface. Coral development is not impressive on the skin of the hull, but is quite lush on much of the modest superstructure. The superstructure and inner hull offer extensive shelter so that groupers, barramundi cod, octopus, and other stealthy creatures can disappear into the ship's interior in an instant.

Meanwhile, when currents flow, I have seen armies of jacks and large turrum attack the surface of the hull, apparently feeding on fish fry. The worse the visibility and the stronger the current, the more marine life we find. I once saw nine groupers, each weighing over 500 pounds, gathered under the bow. There they hovered, in a semicircle, looking in at me with their mouths slowly pumping water over their gills. When approached, they majestically moved off like ships slowly getting up steam.

On other occasions I have sat on the bow and watched flights of eagle rays pass, soaring effortlessly in what was to me a strong current. Batfish, cobia, and barracuda throng in the open water above the *Yongala*, while zebra sharks, sting rays, sea snakes, and turtles are common in its shadow.

Huge schools of jacks, snappers, and sweetlip hover near the bulk of the wreck. There is an unmistakable feeling of shelter and truce as predators and prey seem to mingle; the African water hole has been mentioned as an analogue. Yet, sometimes the mood will abruptly change; large amberjacks or turrum will appear from nowhere to snatch an unwary meal; the truce is shattered by nature's inherent violence. Minutes later, the attack ends as quickly as it began, and once again the lion lies down with the lamb.

The stately butterflyfish (Chelmon rostratus) *can be found on the Great Barrier Reef, but not in great numbers.*

An octopus pauses on a coral head growing atop the bulk of the Yongala *wreck.*

Over the years, the regular traffic of divers has driven away some of the *Yongala*'s denizens. On the other hand, others have become as docile as pets: sting rays, large Napoleon (or Maori) wrasse, and turtles will swim up to you unconcernedly. After all, they have survived thousands of such encounters with humans before.

One problem that persists at the *Yongala* is that divers spend too much time at the 90-foot bottom under the bow or stern. There is a distinct risk of incurring decompression symptoms here; you should at all times be using the decompression tables (or a meter) with great awareness and caution. The marine life is so fascinating that it is easy to lose track of time; a number of divers have gotten themselves into bends problems at the *Yongala* because it is deceptive. After all, who would expect to get into trouble on a wreck that starts at a shallow 45 feet? Yet much of the excitement is at 90 feet, and I have seen divers in trouble whose original plan was to spend the second half of their dive at 45 feet. Somehow the groupers or turtles or rays so fascinated them that they totally forgot their safe dive plan . . .

Given the proper respect, and with a bit of luck on weather and currents, the *Yongala* may give you some of the richest low-visibility dives you'll ever experience.

This stingray is getting ready to swim away.

The author emerges from the Yongala's *interior to come face to face with a ten-foot-long guitar shark* (Rhynchobatus).

Here is one caution in planning your vacation. The best way to see the *Yongala* wreck is as part of a longer itinerary in the Coral Sea. While there are reefs on the Great Barrier Reef that can be combined in a three-day or four-day itinerary, the quality of those reefs may disappoint those who have traveled across the entire Pacific to see Australia's great diving.

At this time, the Cod Hole/Pixie Pinnacle in the north and the *Yongala* wreck in the south are being used in three-day itineraries. While each of these sites are fabulous one-day dive adventures, the diving available to fill out those trips is highly suspect.

Bait Reef (Hayman Island Resort) and the Whitsunday Islands

Typical depth range	:	15-90 feet (5-30 meters)
Typical current conditions	:	None to strong
Expertise required	:	Novice or better
Access	:	Boat

About an hour by fast day-boat from the luxurious Hayman Island Resort is a reef complex known as Bait Reef. Hayman Island and Hamilton Island are major resort complexes of the Whitsunday Islands. The Whitsundays are a wonderful boating area, with many scenic islands, green hills, and fjordlike anchorages. The water is quite turbid, so diving from the resorts is by fast boat or helicopter to sites near the outer rim of the Great Barrier Reef.

Creatures like this fairy basslet who inhabit Pixie Pinnacle are fearless after countless visits by divers.

Bait Reef is a typical example of Great Barrier Reef diving in that its diving quality is quite dependent upon weather and current conditions. I remember taking a dive one day in turbid water with quite a bit of surge, so much so that I spent much of the dive hiding in fissures and canyons looking for close-up subjects. When I returned to the dive boat I discovered that I was the only diver to have completed the dive at all. Later we moved to another area of Bait, where a series of "stepping-stone" reef formations rose to the surface from a bottom at 50 feet. Here the water clarity was a bit better, ranging up to 60 feet.

Reefs such as these are perfectly adequate for snorkelers and brand-new divers who have not seen world-class diving. The dive boat from Hayman Island takes many snorkelers to sites such as the stepping-stones, but serious divers who have traveled from America or Europe will use these reefs only as brief parts of a larger and more exciting Coral Sea itinerary.

Spectacular butterflyfish such as Chaetodon trifasciata *brighten divers' days in the Coral Sea.*

Heron Island

Typical depth range	:	5-60 (2-20 meters)
Typical current condtions	:	None to moderate
Expertise required	:	Novice
Access	:	Boat

Heron, located off the town of Gladstone in the southern Great Barrier Reef, was one of the first resorts to appeal to snorkelers and divers as well as bird-watchers. Heron is very modest in comparison to ambitious resorts such as Hayman or Hamilton Islands, but it has attracted its own audience for a number of years.

Heron's diving is not very different from that offered to clients of Hayman or Hamilton Islands — shallow reef complexes surrounded by passes or canyons whose depths seldom exceed 60 feet.

Tides are very influential here; the time of day when you are scheduled to dive can determine what kind of visibility you will enjoy. Given most hotels' morning schedule of dives, you can therefore encounter visibility ranging from 30-80 feet.

One major dive site, "The Bommie," has been for many years a place to feed the fish. Here, as at the Cod Hole or the *Yongala* wreck, you may be thrilled by the profusion of marine life and accept the visibility, whatever it may be.

A scarlet grouper (Cephalopholis) *rests on a coral colony as it watches for its next meal.*

5

The Northern Coral Sea

Osprey Reef

Typical depth range	: 5-150 (2-50 meters)
Typical current conditions	: None to moderate
Expertise required	: Novice or better
Access	: Boat

Osprey Reef lies some 80 miles north and somewhat eastward of the Cod Hole. It is the most conveniently located of the true Coral Sea reefs, and exhibits both their strengths and weaknesses. Since their strengths are profound and should be treated at some length, I might begin by mentioning weaknesses.

Presently, diving this location involves a long overnight cruise from Cairns (or shorter cruises from Port Douglas or Cooktown) to reach the outer edge of the Great Barrier Reef; and then a second overnight cruise to reach Osprey. For those divers who find the dive sites at Grand Cayman a long haul, this travel could be a deterrent. Of course, it is this same remoteness that has kept Osprey pristine over the years. If it were possible to reach Osprey Reef conveniently it would have been a wasteland long ago. There is not much question that this magnificent reef could easily fall victim to the technology of future decades; in the past 20 years, however, it has been visited infrequently and remains pristine.

While remoteness in miles forms a protective barrier for this grand reef, the fact that those miles are over wide-open sea enhances their effect. This is open ocean. A brisk wind and a long fetch (wind building waves over many miles of open sea) will soon create a very bumpy ride. While some who love exploring find these cruises merely part of exotic diving, other divers prefer to avoid rough, open sea crossings.

That said, a review of Osprey's primary features will explain why most divers find it sublime. Most important is *visibility*. Like other remote Coral

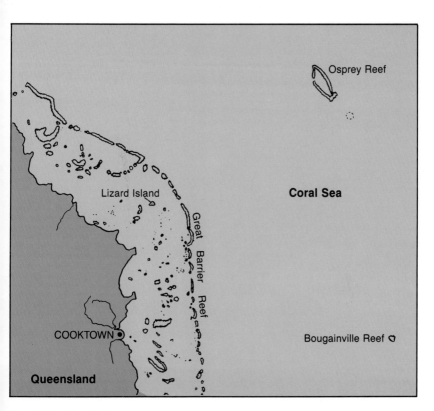

The northern Coral Sea.

Distances

Divers coming to Australia from other parts of the world are seldom prepared for the distances between Australia's attractions. While in the Caribbean one might conceivably dive the best sites within an hour of arrival, Australia might cost you twelve hours of cruising.

The Great Barrier Reef is broad and shallow. Its few good dive sites tend to be at its open-ocean edge. Australia's greatest dive sites are another 80-200 miles further out to sea; out there, great seamounts soar from unimaginable depths to within a few feet of the surface.

To partake of Australia's great diving involves distances and times you will never have encountered before. Not so strangely, the quality of a dive site is often directly related to its distance from any civilization.

Dive boat at anchor off North Horn, at the northern end of Osprey Reef. When the wind is up, this anchorage becomes quite choppy, but during much of the prime season it is flat and calm here.

Sea reefs, Osprey enjoys times when visibility is truly in excess of 200 feet. These periods generally occur between July and December, though they can happen any time. This type of visibility greatly enhances photography. First, of course, one can take pictures of those long vistas of reef; second, shots taken at closer range do not suffer from the "snowfall" that occurs when strobe light illuminates particulate matter in the water. I remember my very first trip to the Coral Sea in October of 1972. The pictures were sensationally crisp and color-drenched. That Christmas I went to Grand Cayman and shot quite a few rolls of film. When it came back from the lab, I was horrified. What had happened to my lenses, or film, or . . . ? Of course, what I was really seeing was the great difference between Caribbean visibility and Coral Sea visibility!

Osprey is an irregular, roughly football-shaped atoll about ten miles long. Because the prevailing winds during the best diving season come from the southeast or east, most of the best dive sites are along the western slopes. There are six major types of dive here, and they recur along the entire western rim of the atoll.

First, there are shallow, exposed coral gardens ranging from 10 to 40 feet in depth. These do not have the lush variety and color of similar reefs in the Philippines or Red Sea because they are dominated by stony corals. Instead they have the raw power of endless statuary, a grand museum of nature's sculpture. The fish that populate these stone flower gardens all seem oversize; indeed, all of them are members of species we see elsewhere in the Indo-Pacific, but here they seem to reach a maturity and size not seen elsewhere. Clown triggerfish, schools of sweetlip, Moorish idols; whatever you see, it will be a major-league specimen. The single dominant type of diving at Osprey and at all of the great Coral Sea reefs is these coral gardens.

A second type of dive is the sheer wall. While there are dropoffs in many parts of Osprey's western rim, most areas drop in stages, with a broad shelf often found at depths of 120-150 feet. However, there are areas just south of the northern tip and just south of the lagoon entrance where the dropoffs are sheer and thrilling. Whenever you have a dramatic

A pair of clownfish (Amphiprion perideraion) *guard their eggs under the mantle of a dazzling anemone.*

Osprey's rim has countless tunnels and byways to dramatically frame a photograph of a diver.

contrast such as intricate stony-coral gardens abruptly plunging over a sheer edge to abyssal depths, you have all the ingredients for dramatic diving. When I dive these precipices, I always have an eye cocked to see what larger citizens might happen by. Manta rays, turtles, orca, large sharks — any of the sea's larger predators might be moving along the wall in the shadowy depths below.

A third type of diving takes place in a series of enormously rewarding canyons (called gutters) through the main rim of the reef. Because the rim corals grow to within a few feet of the surface, these gutters range in depth from 5 to 40 feet. What makes the gutters so unusual is that they are miniature passes through which tidal water flows. As many divers know, when tidal water flows through passes it concentrates a stream of food and marine life develops in great abundance. Soft corals and gorgonian sea whips and sea fans are found in certain of these gutters in overwhelming abundance, so much so that I can remember being in

A *bannerfish* (Heniochus permutatus) *hovers under a ledge and tolerates the approach of divers.*

some fear that my hands or swimfins could be lethal there. The stony walls of the small canyon were completely carpeted with soft-bodied, fragile coral colonies. When these soft corals predominate in a reef setting they signal a locale of rich feeding; it then comes as no surprise to find unusually rich concentrations of reef fish, nudibranchs, starfish, crinoids, and other marine spectaculars in profusion here.

The gutters extend from the interior lagoon all the way through the reef rim to the open sea. Divers may follow them into the lagoon, where a coral rubble bottom is dotted with small pinnacles and shallow reef-lines. Although visibility is somewhat reduced in these enclosed areas (because the open sea cannot flush them clear), you will sometimes find rays, unusual nudibranchs, and many tropical fish amid a rather barren backdrop. Swim through the gutters the opposite way, and fifty yards later you burst out into crystal clear water over stunning depths of open, cobalt-blue sea.

In deeper water, magnificent coral trees in yellow or burgundy stand in silent rows at the edge of the abyss.

In April, 1990, a monstrous cyclone devastated the shallow coral gardens and gutters of Osprey Reef. When I visited in September new life had already begun to bloom; however, the gutters, in particular, were devoid of their former riches. It will take two years to replenish the gutters, and several more years to restore the shallow gardens.

The fourth type of diving is on lateral shelves at depths between 125 and 180 feet. All along Osprey's rim we find coral gardens breaking abruptly to dropoffs, then a shelf of some kind, then a second, steep dropoff to abyssal depths. These shelves may well have been built during the ice ages when water levels were much lower. They are distinguished by low light levels; even in clear water the sunlight is muted at these depths.

It is on these shelves (where they occur) and at similar depths even without shelves that we find the giant soft coral colonies. These immense, fragile colonial structures can be six feet or greater in height. At various atolls in the Coral Sea I have seen them in yellow, burgundy, and even bright pink. These behemoths are absolutely the dominant visual image in their portion of the reef. Their holdfasts may be nearly a foot in diameter, and it is these junctures with the reef that are the huge corals' Achilles heels. Each year when I return another of the giants has fallen away. Apparently a powerful current, combined with the coral's own growing bulk, finally topples these monarchs of the deep reef into the abyss below. A tragedy for those of us who photographically worship them, but merely another event in nature's remorseless time-line.

Osprey's fifth type of dive is at the northern tip of the atoll, known as North Horn. Here the eastern and western rims of the atoll culminate in a sharp point. Below the shallow point is a projecting extension of the point structure at depths of 50-90 feet. On that projecting point (sometimes called the Pulpit) any number of shark feedings have been held, with incredible results.

Manta rays, whale sharks, tuna, schooling barracuda, and other thrilling animals occur here because two currents, moving along the eastern and western rims, meet at North Horn. As so often happens, coral structures projecting over deep water provide funnelling or mixing effects that concentrate food supplies. The point is quite an exposed anchorage, so your boat captain may find great difficulty anchoring when the wind is up.

The five types of diving just described are found at Osprey, and they typify five of the six types of dive sites found at the various Coral Sea atolls.

The sixth variety of dive is the Coral Sea pinnacle, a formation found inside the lagoons of larger atolls such as Flinders, Marion, and Lihou reefs. As I describe reef features at other reefs I will refer back to these elements, the fundamental building blocks of Australia's greatest diving. In the section on Marion where pinnacles are the principal reef feature in the lagoon, they will be discussed in some detail.

A school of barracuda hover silently in open water at North Horn.

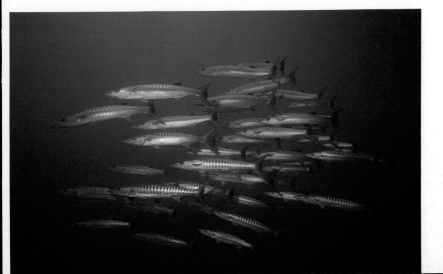

Bougainville Reef

Typical depth range : 5-150 feet (2-50 meters)
Typical current conditions : None to moderate
Expertise required : Novice or better
Access : Boat

While Osprey Reef can be called a medium-sized Coral Sea atoll, Bougainville Reef is one of the smallest examples of the genre. It has a shallow central lagoon, but there is no navigable pass to bring an expeditionary dive cruiser in to anchor. In heavy weather, a boat can anchor within Osprey for a bit of shelter. Bougainville offers only its lee rim. The exposed nature of the entire Coral Sea explains its seasonality. Boat captains are reluctant to venture hundreds of miles out into the open sea where huge cyclones can quickly develop. The combination of no islands or bays in which to shelter, and hundreds of open-water miles to shore,

A diver snorkels into an outer reef rampart of the type found at Osprey, Bougainville, Dart, Flinders, Lihou, and Marion reefs.

Shallow canyons are the ideal breeding grounds for a variety of colorful marine creatures.

reduces the "safe" Coral Sea season to the June-December period, though cruises in January can be fine. While divers chafe when a Coral Sea cruise cannot be scheduled to coincide with their business trip, they surely would not enjoy being on a dive boat in hundred-knot winds and twenty-foot seas.

Interestingly, there are good dive sites on all four sides of the rounded square that is Bougainville's rim. The western rim offers sheer wall, coral garden, and shelf diving similar in many ways to sites at Osprey. In some areas there are also detached pinnacles of coral rising 40-80 feet from a sloping irregular shelf.

The southwestern point is excellent, dropping abruptly to a shelf at 70 feet that begins at the point and continues eastward along the southern rim. Also along the western and southern rims you may find examples of the giant soft corals at depths of 120-130 feet. One cautionary note regarding these brilliant giants: Their mass and fragility make them highly vulnerable to the overweighted or careless diver. Our weight will easily

The Antonio Terrabacchi *wreck lies on the eastern rim of Bougainville Reef.*

This nudibranch (Notodoris) *is nearly six inches long, and moved from one area to another of a large canyon. On the ceiling of a tunnel-like portion of the canyon, the author found the brilliant yellow ribbon of eggs the nudibranch had deposited.*

break their tenuous hold on the sheer reef wall. It goes without saying, then, that divers should be very careful while photographing these giants. We certainly do not want to hasten their inevitable demise.

One unusual dive site distinguishes Bougainville from other Coral Sea reefs. On the eastern rim we can see fragmentary remains of a World War II liberty ship, the *Antonio Terrabacchi*. Actually, little is left above the water, testifying to the extraordinary power of the Coral Sea's storms. On the coral reef rampart, which slopes outward from the rim, major sections of the wreck lie just beneath the surface. During the prime-weather season there are days when the winds shift from southeasterlies to northerlies, then die out. If you arrive at Bougainville on such a day, and if you want a contrast to the western rim, have your captain take you to the wreck. Don't be surprised if he demurs, for anchoring the boat near the wreck is difficult and he may refuse to chance it. The boiler room and shaft lie nearly exposed in clear water, with huge snappers called sweetlip swimming around the massive geometry of the wreck's elements. While this is not beautiful wreck diving such as you would find at Truk Lagoon, it has a raw power to it that provides strong images for your photographs.

6

The Central Coral Sea

While Osprey and Bougainville reefs lie to the north of Cairns, the reefs of the central Coral Sea lie offshore between Cairns and Townsville. In these latitudes we find Holmes, Flora, Dart, Flinders, Moore, Diamond, Lihou, and Abington reefs.

As in the northern Coral Sea, a dive cruiser must first steam through the Great Barrier Reef to reach the open Coral Sea. Looking at a map, we see that a vessel headed for Dart Reef from Townsville might logically stop at Myrmidon. When I visited Myrmidon on such a cruise, I chose it because it projected out from the main reef and I felt that clear water might be enjoyed there.

The Great Barrier Reef's structure is so random, so complex, and so immense that navigating through it in many areas requires that you pick your way visually when the sun is high overhead. When you then reach an outer point such as Myrmidon you are positioned to depart after dinner, steam through the night and arrive at Dart or Flinders reefs early next morning. In my nearly twenty years of offering expeditions to the Coral Sea, reefs such as Myrmidon have offered the very first Australian diving my clients would see. For twenty years, clients have been mildly disappointed in their first Australian dive after coming so far.

Myrmidon is a good example of the Great Barrier Reef diving quality in relation to the Coral Sea reefs. Visibility ranges from 60-80 feet, the corals tend to be somewhat drab, and the marine life is modest. Depths range from some large hills rising to within 30 feet of the surface to valleys of 70-80 feet or more. While Myrmidon does enjoy better visibility than many sites on the Great Barrier Reef, the diver who has flown 6,000 or 9,000 miles and then cruised overnight to reach it may be expecting more.

When the camera moves close to a gorgonian coral colony the astonishing details of its individual polyps become evident. ▶

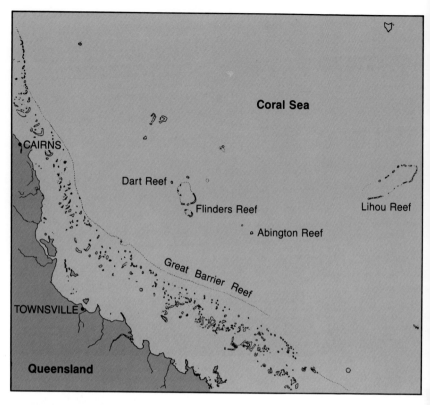

The central Coral Sea.

The good news, of course, is that when you depart Myrmidon and arrive at Flinders the next day you have reached the closest of the true Coral Sea reefs.

At this point it is important to establish quality levels in the Coral Sea. Just as I rate Coral Sea dive sites far higher than most Barrier Reef sites, there are levels of dive quality among the Coral Sea reefs as well.

At the very highest levels I rate certain dives at Osprey, Moore, Abington, Lihou, and Marion reefs. The mid-range of quality would include Bougainville, Flinders, Dart, and Diamond reefs. At the lowest level I would rate Holmes, Flora, and Herald reefs. Please understand that these gradations are all at a comparatively high level; one of the most beautiful soft corals I've ever seen was 140 feet down on the southern slope of Flora. Any one of these reefs will give you some fine dives, but the great ones will give you many dive sites in the world-beater class.

Flinders Reef

Typical depth range : 5-150 feet (2-50 meters)
Typical current conditions : None to strong
Expertise required : Novice or better
Access : Boat

Flinders is one of the largest atolls in the Coral Sea. Its rim is most pronounced at its northern and southern extremities. It is one of three atolls (with Marion and Lihou) that are exceptional in having good to superb diving on coral pinnacles within their large lagoons.

Most lagoon structures in the Pacific are semiclosed systems. Tidal water flows in and out through limited openings called passes; this produces characteristic currents in the passes and (almost always) turbid water trapped in the lagoon.

These Coral Sea atolls, on the other hand, are wide open. No more than half of their rims are fully erect; thus there is no obstacle to massive tidal flow, and crystal clear ocean water flushes the lagoons at will.

A dive cruiser is brilliant in the sun, just a few feet above a large anemone.

In the lagoons, the bottom is flat sand and coral rubble, and for some reason nature has seeded, seemingly at random, huge towers or pinnacles of coral which rise nearly to the surface. These pinnacles can occur as monolithic, single towers nearly 200 feet tall, or there can be ten or more towers close together on a large plateau, with sand or rubble-filled valleys between the towers at depths of 50-70 feet.

The coral pinnacles are covered with a surface of beautiful living corals, including some impressively developed *Turbinaria*, a yellow, scalloped coral. Standing alone in the open lagoon water, these towers become a gathering-place for an incredible kaleidoscope of marine life. I have watched schools of rainbow runners, or tuna, or horse-eyed jacks wheel slowly against a backdrop of open cobalt-blue ocean.

Steaming into Flinders after a night crossing the open Coral Sea, we see one of the few pieces of real estate in the entire Coral Sea. At the southern entrance to the lagoon lies a small sandbar island perhaps 100 yards in length and permanent enough to have a small electronic weather station. Extending southward from the sandbar is a linear reef cut with deep cross-channels, plunging on its western face into deep water. To the diver, the result is a series of tall towers of coral separated by 60-foot gashes.

Water Clarity and Visibility

Australia's remote Coral Sea reefs are frequently blessed with water clarity seldom equalled anywhere on the globe. Why is the water so clear? Essentially, because there are no landmasses, no rivers, no shallow reef complexes such as the Great Barrier Reef anywhere nearby.

There are, on occasion, open-water plankton blooms, which reduce visibility. In addition, strong tides sometimes bring turbid water from the lagoons out over the dropoffs.

As is true anywhere in the world, the visibility you encounter on your own cruise to the Coral Sea will involve some luck. No one has been able to predict visibility beyond the fact that it is frequently excellent. Typical Coral Sea lateral visibility will be 150 feet; if your luck is good you might see for 200 feet or more.

◄

An example of the legendary Coral Sea visibility: When conditions are right, you may experience the best visibility of your diving career.

Feeding gorgonian fans soften nature's craggy coral valleys.

Immediately inside the southern lagoon entrance on the western side are several freestanding pinnacles. When the weather is calm these pinnacles can practically gleam in the sun and visibility can exceed 200 feet. On one expedition we had some cameras leak at one site; it subsequently become known as the Jinx Bommie. That incident indicates once again how you may hear various names for dive sites, yet later find other local experts respond blankly to your inquiry. This was "Jinx Bommie" to *those* divers on *that* boat *that* day . . . Jinx had a double top with a valley between, sheer sides, and a huge rose-colored soft coral colony at its western base.

North of Jinx perhaps two miles away lies a large plateau with several pinnacles clustered together, separated by narrow valleys some 60 feet deep. These valleys or canyons funnel tidal water such that impressive concentrations of yellow gorgonian corals grow here. Some of these fans will grow up to ten feet across, silently feeding in an invisible food stream. As if touched by King Midas, phalanxes of golden-yellow fans line the canyon walls, one after the other. Silent sentinels, they forever keep watch on the valley, while occasional manta rays, sharks, or turtles glide softly through the valley as if passing in review.

Some of the coral pinnacles within the southeastern rim of Flinders are swept by currents of 2-3 knots. Many of them are covered with thousands of crinoids (feather starfish), which have remained morphologically unchanged for 400 million years. Crinoids cluster where currents flow over shallow reefs in bright sunlight. They contrast totally with soft corals, which shun bright light and are found in deeper water or under shadowed ledges.

◄

One of the most prolific families in the Coral Sea is that of the crinoid, or feather starfish (Comanthina). These complex animals have remained virtually unchanged for 400 million years.

Dart Reef

Typical depth range	:	5-150 feet (2-50 meters)
Typical current conditions	:	None to strong
Expertise required	:	Novice or better
Access	:	Boat

North and west of Flinders lies a towering reef known as Dart. Unlike Flinders, Dart is a solid tower of coral rising from the depths and stopping abruptly just beneath the surface. The top of this truncated tower is perhaps a mile across, and it glitters like some aquamarine jewel under the tropical sun.

Dart's flanks are nearly vertical, so much so that ocean-going dive boats must literally drop their anchors on top of the reef: Don't drop your camera as you leave the dive platform; it's a *long* way down.

At the eastern end of Dart lies the Long Valley. This structure is an L-shaped, broad, sandy area some 50-70 feet deep. Along its northern edge are coral ramparts that rise to the surface, while a low coral reef rises a mere 10-15 feet along its southern edge.

A snorkeler peers down at a Coral Sea pinnacle in near-perfect conditions.

In the open water above isolated pinnacles, one finds schools of pelagic fish in shallow water; these sleek hunters seem to be taking a social break from their lifelong hunt.

Beyond the southern edge is a steep dropoff. If you dive in the valley, currents which enter from the east make it a natural food channel. A good-sized school of barracuda and a school of jacks are regularly found here. The jacks slowly migrate over the hills and through the valleys that mark the eastern limit of Dart. These are magical moments, soaring with these great silver fish that always look surprised. If the divers are relaxed the school will sometimes remain for quite a while; there are few more exhilarating moments a human visitor can enjoy.

At the western end of the valley a sand channel turns at right angles and plunges down the outer, southern face of Dart. West of this sand channel at 140-160 feet are dozens of huge soft coral colonies and some very large gorgonian fans.

Sometimes a ten-foot silvertip shark comes to visit. Silvertip sharks in the Coral Sea tend to be what the Australians call "cheeky." That means they will buzz you just to see if your adrenal glands are working. It can be some fun, but the sharks are really only curious.

Upon leaving Dart you will pass Herald's Surprise. Despite its colorful name, which conjures up visions of Captain Herald's vessel high and dry, the diving I saw there was rather poor. Having spent a twenty-year career exploring reefs before other divers got to them, I can assure you that being the first to go places is a mixed bag. Sometimes one studies the charts, sees a reef, and discovers a treasure; other times one travels for hours, drops the

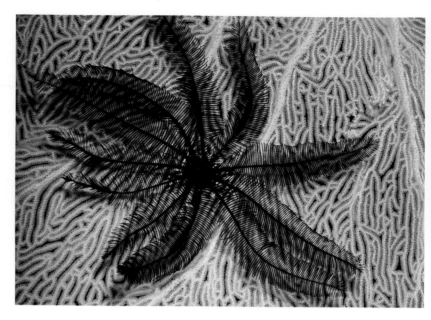

A jet-black crinoid arrays itself on a golden gorgonian to achieve a favored position in a food-bearing current.

anchor, and finds barren reefs. This certainly illustrates how crucial a knowledgeable captain can be on a dive cruise. His understanding of tides, currents, and weather can make all the difference.

In the Coral Sea, only a handful of captains know where to find the great reef sites, and for a very good reason. It is very expensive to run large dive boats over thousands of miles of ocean to reach the reefs. Even the top captains only get out to the oceanic reefs a few times each year. If and when they go, they have clients on board. They can't afford to dive any poor sites, so they tend to repeat the anchorages they know are good. All of this helps you realize why it is risky to think of Australia in terms of your past experience on Caribbean islands.

A long overnight steam to the east is Diamond Shoals. Diamond is a broad plateau without spectacular features, but it does lie on the crossing path to Lihou and Marion. An important consideration in laying out a cruise itinerary is to have travel limited to overnight journeys so as to leave the days for diving. Thus, places such as Diamond can be handy for captains planning their cruises.

Diamond does have a small island and associated reefs on its southeastern rim. The island covers perhaps two acres and is half wooded, half sand. In the low scrub brush of the wooded part, thousands of terns, kingfishers,

Near Diamond Island, a shoaling reef attracts goatfish, bream, and other species in clear water.

and gannets nest. The cacophony that starts when you go ashore not only would raise the dead but send them running!

The sandy half of the island attracts nesting green sea turtles *(Chelonia mydas)*, 300-500 pound leviathans lumbering ashore in the darkness. During afternoon dives in the October nesting season the sight of turtles copulating in stacks of up to three individuals can give one pause.

Off the island is a sandy shallows running out across the shoals. The sandy bottom at 30-50 feet is punctuated by scattered patch reefs rising 20-40 feet from the sand. Often large nurse sharks or turtles will rest on the sand, while a school of tuna or a massive tiger shark can take you by surprise in the valleys.

One patch reef reaches the surface and lies awash. The churning of the gin-clear water about its crown seems to attract a goodly number of fish to swarm about this structure. Schools of dozens to hundreds of grunts, goatfish, and other species hover in what look very much like purely social gatherings.

Diamond is, however, at best a way station. From the island you are positioned for an overnight to Marion to the southeast, Lihou to the east, or even Moore to the north.

Before I treat those three, however, let me describe for you an alternate way station we can use on our way to Marion Reef.

Abington Reef

Typical depth range	:	5-150 feet (2-50 meters)
Typical current conditions	:	None to strong
Expertise required	:	Novice or better
Access	:	Boat

If the weather is very calm you can travel via Abington Reef, a tiny pinnacle of coral in an otherwise empty sea. Abington provides excellent diving, but is too small to offer any protection or overnight anchorage in the event of rough weather.

Abington's most important features for divers are a series of coral towers lying to the south of its western point. Out here in the crystal waters of the Coral Sea a tiny structure such as Abington enjoys stunning clarity for most of the prime season. The coral towers lie perhaps 20-50 yards off the main flat-topped mass of the reef; their seaward sides plunge down into depths of 6,000 feet. If there were some large atoll like Flinders or Marion nearby for anchorage, Abington would be dived more often. As it is, once in a while a combination of good weather and dive cruise schedule allows a day here.

Small reef fish live by browsing on coral polyps. Butterflyfish such as Chaetodon falcula *must have few natural enemies, for they appear to be quite defenseless.*

Lihou Reef

Typical depth range	:	5-150 feet (2-50 meters)
Typical current conditions	:	None to strong
Expertise required	:	Novice or better
Access	:	Boat

The latest of the central Coral Sea atolls to be seriously dived, Lihou is most similar to Marion in its basic structure. Its outer rim is open all along the western side, forming an immense crescent of shallow reef with a partial interior lagoon sheltered from weather by its eastern outer rim. Clear ocean water circulates freely in the lagoon, and there are scattered pinnacles like those of Marion and Flinders. Along the southern outer rim grow those immense soft coral colonies that populate even the smallest Coral Sea reefs.

In considering Lihou and Marion Reefs as our final two "big" reefs, it is first proper to speculate about the distinguishing feature they share. The interior pinnacles of Flinders, Lihou, and Marion make them different from any similar-seeming structures elsewhere in the world.

The reefs are honeycombed with grottos and caverns where fish laze. Year after year one can find what appear to be the same fish at the same sites.

Pilotfish manage to ride the bow wave on the nose of a speeding shark.

These awesome towers of coral in crystal water are almost surely a product of subsidence, the slow migration and sinking of tectonic plates. It was the visionary Charles Darwin who postulated that the only way to create an atoll was to have a volcanic mountain sink into the sea. It was nearly a hundred years before Darwin was vindicated, through undersea observations by a submarine captain named Harry Hess.

When volcanoes sink (because the plates beneath them subside) a delicate balance sometimes occurs. If the rate of subsidence approximately balances with the upward growth of corals, a circular or oval coral reef gradually becomes that "trademark" empty ring we call an atoll.

Now, if you visualize that process, the pinnacles are no mystery. Every inner lagoon has scattered coral heads across an otherwise barren bottom. At Lihou and other Coral Sea reefs there was clearly tidal water circulating a rich food supply. These scattered coral colonies, like the fringing reef around them, grew upward toward the sunlight. In time, the lagoon floor sank (and is still sinking to this day) such that the growing coral structures rise nearly 200 feet from the present bottom.

From our selfish human perspective, nature's handiwork is just what we would have ordered. The strong tidal currents provide sizeable passes into and out of the lagoon; thus the corals and other invertebrates feed well and flourish. At the same time (unlike most lagoons) this flushing action brings the crystal-clear waters of the open sea into these fabled lagoons.

Each of these three reefs have so many of these sublime structures that no one has even come close to exploring them all. With luck, they will last for many years without human depredation.

One careless human act could eradicate any one of these grandest of the world's reefs. Dynamiting, long-lines, or trawl nets could destroy nature's handiwork, slowly grown over millenia. Over the years I have seen several of my personal "top ten" best dive sites destroyed. These would be the greatest loss of all.

Lihou's pinnacles, like those of Marion and Flinders, are a riot of yellow *Turbinaria* coral colonies, flourishing crinoids, timid batfish, and open-water schooling species. When you swim through a valley between pinnacles, you

This clownfish (Amphiprion perideraion) is guarding its tiny orange eggs.

Jessica Roessler discovers an immense, lazy nurse shark sleeping in a sand valley between two pinnacles.

never know when you might chance upon a sleeping ray, or a huge nurse shark, or even a beautiful spotted zebra shark *(Stegastoma)*. You really must be prepared to find anything around the next corner, and there are literally hundreds of corners.

For photographers, Lihou's pinnacles and outer walls require the ability to shift mental gears quickly; at one moment you may be studying a nudibranch, moments later maneuvering in open water with a large ray or turtle or shark. Indeed, this is the essence of diving in the Coral Sea. We study the smaller creatures as we move about the reef, yet at each turn we hope for a pulse-pounding encounter with one of the large animals.

Sharks

The Coral Sea reefs have sharks as natural residents. These reefs represent one of the world's best opportunities to get photos of sharks.

Sharks are extremely sensitive to noise, scent, and disturbance. Often, the first divers to enter the water see sharks, while later entrants see none. The sharks merely drift away to darker, deeper, and quieter water until the disruptive divers leave.

There are certain sites where a dozen or more sharks seem to be in constant residence. North Horn at Osprey Reef and Action Point at Marion Reef have had resident sharks for the nearly twenty years we have been diving there.

Many species of sharks can be seen: grays, silvertips, tigers, hammerheads, reef whitetips, zebra sharks, nurse sharks, and even the small nocturnal epaulette shark.

From pinnacle to pinnacle across open water is a half-mile or less, but finding the next tower can be very difficult without either radar bearings or a satellite fix. We have found some of our best pinnacles by pure dumb luck: proceeding from A to B and stumbling upon C somewhere between the two known sites.

One interesting distinction Lihou has is that its shark population has not yet been impacted by any significant diver traffic. Over the years I have seen the sharks retreat from dive sites that were visited even ten days per year. The sharks grimly cling to certain sites such as Action Point at Marion and North Horn at Osprey; even at North Horn they have moved deeper to avoid humans, and return only when a feeding takes place.

Even in the early days we noticed that only the first few divers in the water saw sharks at the pinnacles. As soon as the first divers spread out the sharks disappeared. Was it our noise? Was it the fact that noisy divers simply took away privacy and stealth? For whatever reason, pinnacles that once had brief shark encounters to offer no longer have them.

7

The Southern Coral Sea

Marion Reef

Typical depth range	:	5-150 feet (2-50 meters)
Typical current conditions	:	None to strong
Expertise required	:	Novice or better
Access	:	Boat

Marion Reef is one of the world's most remarkable places for divers. My first cruise out there was in 1972, and I have made a dozen or more cruises since.

The hard-coral statuary of a Coral Sea reef-top is enhanced by the clarity of the surrounding water.

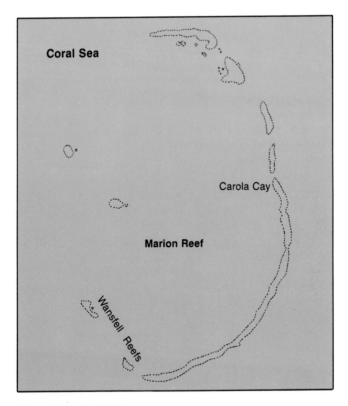

The southern Coral Sea.

This is a classic atoll some thirteen miles by seven miles, with its eastern rim intact and western rim intermittent. The floor of the lagoon is 150-200 feet deep, and some of the most beautiful coral structures anywhere grow there. The words "coral structures" do not do justice to these spectacular pinnacles soaring from the floor of the lagoon to the surface.

Unlike most lagoons, which contain murky water, Marion's lagoon water is as clear as the open ocean around it. As we cruise across the cobalt blue water, here and there a small patch of aquamarine can be seen. These daubs of color mark the upper extremities of the pinnacles. If you arrive on a gray day with high clouds, it can be almost impossible to see (and therefore find) these coral towers.

There are no charts of the pinnacles. Two boat captains have found and taken satellite navigation fixes or radar locations on a number of pinnacles; unfortunately, this information is closely guarded because those captains invested a great deal of time and money to glean it. Moreover, under these circumstances, the names given to the fifty or more sets of pinnacles are entirely arbitrary. Names such as Number 7, Number 8, and Number 9 don't tell you much; Tigertank and The Seven Sisters don't either. There are a few, such as Carl's Supreme, named for certain worthies who were aboard when those particular pinnacles were first discovered.

Here are some instructive generalities about the pinnacles. First, they seem to be located in completely random locations; there is no plan or pattern. Second, most rise to within ten feet or less of the surface, so once you are anchored, access is very easy. Third, you may find a single vertical tower such as Number 9, a pair of joined towers such as Tigertank, or a plateau with several towers such as the Seven Sisters. There seems to be a tendency at Marion for plateaus with groups of pinnacles to be found on the eastern side of the lagoon, while the more widely scattered single towers are further west.

At the plateau formations, the several towers have sand-filled canyons between them where large nurse sharks, rays, turtles, and groupers rest. On the towers themselves the outer "skin" is composed of live corals, while the central mass is composed of the limestone skeletons of astronomical numbers of coral polyps long dead. Considering what a tiny limestone cup each coral polyp builds during its lifetime, these mountains of limestone bespeak nature's endless patience in building her monuments.

As dive sites, the pinnacles of Marion offer great contrasts to the Great Barrier Reef, and when one is diving out here the distinctions are vivid. First and foremost is the clarity of the open-ocean water. Second is the fact that pelagic species such as tuna, rainbow runners, jacks, sharks, and rays seem to come to these tower complexes to rest or socialize after hunting. Perhaps the towers serve as reference or rendezvous points for these open-ocean roamers: "Hey, guys, let's go fishing and then all meet back at Number Nine. . . ."

Third is the coincidence that a bright yellow scalloped coral, *Turbinaria*, is very common at Marion. In the bright sunlight and clear water the yellow adds flair to the overall look of the reef.

And then there are the sea snakes. For various reasons the range of the half-dozen species of sea snakes only extends as far north as Marion. Flinders and Lihou reefs bear a topographical resemblance to Marion, but the snakes make Marion unique.

Sea snakes, like other marine creatures, suffer from a vile reputation which is mostly mythology. Yes, it is true that sea snakes are equipped with venom far more powerful than that of terrestrial cobras. Having said that, most of the rest of what you normally hear is nonsense. For one thing, sea snakes

Typically large gorgonian fans in a canyon between two tall pinnacles. ▶

The business end of a four-foot-long olive sea snake resting on the reef.

are gentle, curious creatures who spend most of their time rolled in hoops on the sea floor, sound asleep. When they stir every hour or so, it is to make a leisurely journey to the surface for a breath. After twenty years of watching divers and snakes, I have noticed that it is the snakes' swimming to the surface that scares the socks off divers. The snakes simply *look* lethal, and the divers' imaginations run wild.

When, as often happens with a curious creature, the snake alters course to swim toward the diver, pandemonium reigns. In fact, the snake is thinking something like, "My word! what a strange looking apparition. I must take a closer look." Meanwhile, the diver is imagining the snake as some messenger from Lucifer. This can lead to one of the most hysterical ballets in the sea; the diver backpedals furiously, fins churning the water. The snake gets caught in the roiling water and is tumbled wildly. The human thinks the snake is pressing its ultimate attack; the snake is having a ball in a wild amusement park ride. What we have here is a failure to communicate . . .

One final note: Snakes love shiny things such as your wristwatch, decompression meters, cameras, and glass faceplates. I have watched a snake flick

Sea Snakes

Sea snakes are among the most misunderstood creatures in the sea. Their reputation as lethally-armed killers is a product of hyperactive human imagination.

The facts are these:

1. These sea-going relatives of the terrestrial cobra are air-breathers (who can hold a breath for up to two hours), and do have small fangs connected to sacs of lethal poison.
2. However, their jaws are exceedingly fragile. They hunt by night, reaching into holes and injecting fish with their poison. The fish die without a struggle, and are swallowed whole by the snake.
3. Far from being monsters, the snakes are lethargic lay-abouts by day. If you do happen upon them when they wake up to go to the surface to breathe, they will sometimes become very curious about your shiny cameras, gauges, meters, and facemasks. They rush to flick their tongues on these bright items, and divers mistake curiosity for aggression.
4. In truth, these gentle, curious creatures will be a highlight of your diving at Marion Reef or the *Yongala* wreck. They are rarely found any further north.

Sea snakes are *lethally armed, but usually good-natured.*

A passing shark eyes a group of divers as a shark-feeding is prepared.

its tiny forked tongue over every inch of an underwater camera. The owner, frozen in apprehension if not fear, spent minute after minute expecting to be bitten, while violence was clearly the farthest thing from the snake's mind.

Another creature whose reputation is built on fearful overimagination is the shark. The joy of Australia's Coral Sea is that you see sharks on almost every dive. Parenthetically, I must say that the publishing of this guide could signal the end of that era; too many visiting divers will directly cause the sharks to go elsewhere.

A shark is just another fish unless you purposely induce a feeding situation. At Marion Reef there are four special shark spots, places we go specifically in hopes of good shark photography.

The first is Action Point, at the northern end of Marion. Since 1972 I have never made a trip here without there being at least a dozen gray sharks, some huge groupers, and occasionally a hammerhead or silvertip shark. This is where we have put on dozens of shark feedings. They have been very instructive, and almost always divers come away far less frightened of sharks.

In general, I find that sharks are like dogs. In packs, and when they are competing for food, they can become aggressive. Still, they are like dogs, and can usually be faced down by a determined human.

As the sharks get larger the equation naturally shifts, but only the great white shark (which I have never seen in the Coral Sea) is so large as to cause concern. On one occasion, a fifteen-foot hammerhead arrived at the conclusion of a shark feeding. After several "close encounters" with what indeed looked like a mother ship, I gave the shark the food I was holding. In retrospect it was clear to me that if sharks were the death machines they have been portrayed as, I would never have returned from the encounter. I did return, therefore at least with *that* shark on *that* day my benign theory of shark behavior was vindicated. I try not to hang my life on that theory very often, but it has worked each time so far.

The crucial thing to understand about sharks is that they are not vengeful murder machines. They are just out to feed themselves as easily as possible. Determined resistance is precisely what they do not want, and they will often look elsewhere for food if you convince them that messing around with you will provoke retaliation. Fortunately, the sharks do not know how hollow a threat we are . . .

A second "shark spot" visiting divers usually don't see is the pass south of Carola Cay. Here one may encounter seventeen-foot hammerheads, but the currents can be strong. Some professional film crews have worked here, but it is generally not a place for vacation diving.

The third and fourth shark centers are found at the northern and southern ends of Wansfell Reef. Wansfell lies in the southwestern quadrant of Marion. Currents flow here that may generally elevate the marine life around this reef mass; or, perhaps it is simply a way station or navigation beacon for ocean-going sharks. I can vividly remember swimming north-ward along a shallow ridge only to come face to face with a twelve-foot tiger shark. The two of us did an elaborate "After you, Alphonse," "Oh, no, after *you,* Gaston," and passed without incident.

Before leaving Marion Reef it is only fair to point out that some areas of the lagoon have poor circulation. Visibility is reduced, and the diving is rather weak just inside the southeastern rim, because that rim is quite intact. These areas do, however, offer the only protected anchorage when the wind comes up, and that is the only reason we have ever dived them.

As I leave Marion Reef with its many adventures I pause to read some of the brief notes I made on a cruise there. Sadly, these pinnacle names were given by a captain who is no longer even in the business. The notes read:

- Number 8 is the needle. Sheer sides, clear water, Wow!
- Number 7 is excellent, but best of all is the lonely pinnacle off SW end of cluster. Giant soft coral south end where I saw turtle.

At Wansfell Reef (a portion of Marion Reef) a graceful green sea turtle slows as it senses the presence of unknown intruders.

- Radar pinnacle excellent – Rays – tip has many crinoids at 80 feet, looks down on sand and turtle rock.
- Number 7 superb. Big nurse shark, saddle formation with three big anemones, two nice small bommies with resident zebra shark, tuna circling.
- Newfound near Radar really untouched, steep valleys, golden fans, red gorgonians, yellow anemones.
- Reef inside Wansfell nice. Two silvertip sharks, big school of turrum (a large species of jack).
- Carl's Supreme – Hammerhead, good snakes on two southernmost pinnacles.

- New bommie near Number 8 very nice. Go all the way around to the valley of fans.
- Tigertank sensational – schooling rainbow runners, circling tuna, cuttlefish, reef fish.
- Number 10 is sublime, has everything, whitetip shark came many times.
- Number 4 – excellent. Good turtle, grouper in canyon, adult and baby nudibranch.
- South of Number 10. New pinnacle is big. Has everything!

For a final comment on Marion, which I still consider one of the two best places in the world to dive, I would say: To get the most out of these great pinnacles, be prepared to swim. The more area you cover, the more you will see. If your target is the larger animals this is especially

Anemones grow to massive size in the Coral Sea. This example of Radianthus ritteri *is symbiotically inhabited by a family of clownfish* (Amphiprion perideraion).

A sweetlip (Gaterin diagrammus) *allows a cleaner wrasse to pluck parasites from its open mouth.*

true. Wandering up and down the canyons will sooner or later bring you face to face with huge groupers, nurse sharks, rays, turtles, and gray sharks. The sedentary divers who stay under the anchored boat can miss a lot at Marion or any other of the sublime Coral Sea reefs.

One of the greatest cruises I ever had out there was with a former University of Illinois competitive swimmer who challenged me: No matter how far we swam, he wanted big animals. We must have covered ten miles in ten days, but did we find adventure!

Marion's great, untouched reefs have remained pristine since 1972. When a treasure like this is protected only by distance, it seems inevitable that some vandal will find and pillage it. Marion, Lihou, and other Coral Sea reefs should be protected by National Park status, as is much of the Great Barrier Reef. If we are lucky, protective status will be achieved and the personal notes I cited above will trumpet for generations of divers. If not, they will echo sadly as requiem for these and other great reefs.

Their fate is in our hands.

8

Marine Life of Australia

The marine life of Australia is among the richest and most varied in the world. Every major family of Pacific fish and invertebrate is represented, often with spectacular examples.

The Great Barrier Reef, whatever its visibility and current problems for photographers, is a great breeding ground for marine species. One of my favorite statistics is that, while there are twelve species of damselfish in the Caribbean, there are ninety-two just on the Great Barrier Reef. Dozens of species of butterflyfish dazzle the eye, while groupers, snappers, angelfish, parrotfish, and other local citizens congregate on the reefs. Several hundred species of coral inhabit Australia, and in the turbid, plankton-filled waters of the Great Barrier Reef they have built monumental edifices of limestone. Around these great structures fish throng, feeding on the live coral polyps which make up the skin surface of the massive ramparts.

Some years ago we used to dive the Swains Group in the southern Great Barrier Reef near Rockhampton, where photography tended to be limited because of the turbidity, but the marine life was extraordinarily prolific. Indeed, one sees similar hothouse conditions in turbid reef areas of the Philippines, Solomons, and New Guinea as well. Scalloped corals, dome corals, brain corals, branching corals, and soft corals cover literally every inch of available substrate.

Of course, this abundance of coral is a wonderfully rich feeding area for fish. We find the browsing coral-eaters such as parrotfish, wrasse, and butterflyfish in great abundance, groupers ranging from coral cod to the homely barramundi cod, barracuda, a variety of sharks, rays, and turtles; even whale sharks, pilot whales, and dolphins are commonly seen.

If the Great Barrier Reef is so blessed with life, why not just dive there and forget the distant Coral Sea reefs? What (other than visibility) is the real difference? First, the visibility is crucial, because in the Coral Sea you can *see* creatures which might pass undetected on the Barrier Reef. Second, while marine creatures are more widely scattered on the open-ocean atolls, the ones that are there tend to be larger than life. When you see a giant soft coral, a tiger shark, a Maori wrasse, even a Moorish idol

A large lionfish (Pterois volitans) *flares silently at the base of a reef.*

or a grouper, it will be the biggest, fattest, sassiest one you have ever seen. Whenever I think of Australia and the Coral Sea, I see it as in every way the ultimate dive experience. It is the place where a whale shark comes right to the dive boat, where manta rays wander in the shallow canyons, where soft corals grow six feet tall, where entire caves filled with radiant soft corals and gorgonians await the explorer.

There are extravagant canary-yellow nudibranchs several inches long, immense helmet conch, brilliant blood-red or blue starfish *(Linckia)* two feet across, sweetlip (snappers) with cleaner wrasse cleaning inside their mouths; even a random list is a tapestry of color and awe.

In the end, mere words cannot describe the diving out in the Coral Sea. I remember one day standing on a shallow coral pinnacle with visibility that must have been 300 feet. I gave up trying to take pictures and just stared like some mountain climber at the world below. Over there a shark, in another direction a ray, spread out over an immense landscape. Anywhere else in the world, those creatures would have passed me by, but in this extraordinary place I could be like the eye of God seeing everything.

The Moorish idol is a striking study in black and white. ▶

Appendix: Great Barrier Reef and Coral Sea Dive Services*

* The list below is included as a service to the reader. The author has made every effort to make this list complete at the time this book was printed. This list does not constitute an endorsement of these operators and dive shops.

The Coral Sea Live-Aboard Dive Cruiser

Pacific Thunder (Premiere Live-Aboard in the Coral Sea)
50 Francisco Street, Suite 205
San Francisco, CA 94133
1-800-PAC-DIVE

M.V. Hero
50 Francisco St., Suite 205
San Francisco, CA 94133
1-800-PAC-DIVE

M.V. Reef Explorer
50 Francisco St., Suite 205
San Francisco, CA 94133
1-800-PAC-DIVE

Mixed Great Barrier Reef and Coral Sea Diving Cruises

Mike Ball Watersports
c/o See & Sea Travel, Inc.
50 Francisco Street, Suite 205
San Francisco, CA 94133
1-800-DIV-XPRT
1-415-434-3400

S. Y. Scheherezade
50 Francisco Street, Suite 205
San Francisco, CA 94133
1-800-DIV-XPRT

Hotels and Boats Offering the Great Barrier Reef

Lizard Island, Dunk Island, Brampton Island, and Bedarra Island
Comer, Hunter & Phillips St.
Chefley Square
Sydney NSW 2000
FAX 011-61-2-231-1959

Australian Airlines Resort Islands — Dunk, Brampton, Bedarra

Quicksilver Diving Service (Day trips only)
Marina Mirage Shop #12
Port Douglas QLD 4871
FAX (070) 99 5525
TEL. (070) 99 5050

Heron Island (P & O Resorts)
482 Kingsford Smith Drive
Brisbane QLD 4001
FAX (070) 268 8220
TEL. (070) 268 8224

Hayman Island
Great Barrier Reef
North Queensland
TEL. (079) 46 9100

Coral Sea Diving Services
(Day trips)
P.O. Box 122
Port Douglas QLD 4871
FAX (070) 99 3384
TEL. (070) 98 5254

Nimrod III
155 Sheridan Street
Cairns QLD 4870
FAX (070) 31 1373
TEL. (070) 31 1288

Diver Guidelines for Protecting Reefs*

1. Maintain proper buoyancy control, and avoid over-weighting.
2. Use correct weight belt position to stay horizontal, i.e., raise the belt above your waist to elevate your feet/fins, and move it lower toward your hips to lower them.
3. Use your tank position in the backpack as a balance weight, i.e., raise your backpack on the tank to lower your legs, and lower the backpack on the tank to raise your legs.
4. Watch for buoyancy changes during a dive trip. During the first couple of days, you'll probably breathe a little harder and need a bit more weight than the last few days.
5. Be careful about buoyancy loss at depth; the deeper you go the more your wet suit compresses, and the more buoyancy you lose.
6. Photographers must be extra careful. Cameras and equipment affect buoyancy. Changing f-stops, framing a subject, and maintaining position for a photo often conspire to prohibit the ideal "no-touch" approach on a reef. So, when you must use "holdfasts," choose them intelligently.
7. Avoid full leg kicks when working close to the bottom and when leaving a photo scene. When you inadvertently kick something, stop kicking! Seems obvious, but some divers either semi-panic or are totally oblivious when they bump something.
8. When swimming in strong currents, be extra careful about leg kicks and handholds.
9. Attach dangling gauges, computer consoles, and octopus regulators. They are like miniature wrecking balls to a reef.
10. Never drop boat anchors onto a coral reef.

---

*Condensed from "Diver Guidelines" by Chris Newbert ©Oceanica 1991.

Index

Let these Pisces Diving and Snorkeling Guides show you the underwater wonders of —

9578